MAD LIBS®
ESCAPE FROM DETENTION
MAD LIBS

I will not play Mad Libs in class.
I will not play Mad Libs in class.
I will not play Mad Libs in class.
I will not play Mad Libs in class.
I will not play

concept created by Roger Price & Leonard Stern

PSS!
PRICE STERN SLOAN
An Imprint of Penguin Group (USA)

PRICE STERN SLOAN
Published by the Penguin Group
Penguin Group (USA), 375 Hudson Street, New York, New York 10014, USA

USA | Canada | UK | Ireland | Australia | New Zealand | India | South Africa | China
Penguin Books Ltd, Registered Offices: 80 Strand, London WC2R 0RL, England

For more information about the Penguin Group visit penguin.com

Published by Price Stern Sloan,
a division of Penguin Young Readers Group,
345 Hudson Street, New York, New York 10014.

ISBN 978-0-8431-7379-6

1 3 5 7 9 10 8 6 4 2

MAD LIBS
INSTRUCTIONS

MAD LIBS® is a game for people who don't like games! It can be played by one, two, three, four, or forty.

• RIDICULOUSLY SIMPLE DIRECTIONS

In this tablet you will find stories containing blank spaces where words are left out. One player, the READER, selects one of these stories. The READER does not tell anyone what the story is about. Instead, he/she asks the other players, the WRITERS, to give him/her words. These words are used to fill in the blank spaces in the story.

• TO PLAY

The READER asks each WRITER in turn to call out a word—an adjective or a noun or whatever the space calls for—and uses them to fill in the blank spaces in the story. The result is a MAD LIBS® game.

When the READER then reads the completed MAD LIBS® game to the other players, they will discover that they have written a story that is fantastic, screamingly funny, shocking, silly, crazy, or just plain dumb—depending upon which words each WRITER called out.

• EXAMPLE (*Before* and *After*)

"_____!" he said _____
　　　　EXCLAMATION　　　　　　　　　　　　　ADVERB

as he jumped into his convertible _____ and
　　　　　　　　　　　　　　　　　　　　NOUN

drove off with his _____ wife.
　　　　　　　　ADJECTIVE

"_____*Ouch*_____!" he said _____*stupidly*_____
　　　EXCLAMATION　　　　　　　　　　　　　ADVERB

as he jumped into his convertible _____*cat*_____ and
　　　　　　　　　　　　　　　　　　　NOUN

drove off with his _____*brave*_____ wife.
　　　　　　　　ADJECTIVE

In case you have forgotten what adjectives, adverbs, nouns, and verbs are, here is a quick review:

An ADJECTIVE describes something or somebody. *Lumpy, soft, ugly, messy,* and *short* are adjectives.

An ADVERB tells how something is done. It modifies a verb and usually ends in "ly." *Modestly, stupidly, greedily,* and *carefully* are adverbs.

A NOUN is the name of a person, place, or thing. *Sidewalk, umbrella, bridle, bathtub,* and *nose* are nouns.

A VERB is an action word. *Run, pitch, jump,* and *swim* are verbs. Put the verbs in past tense if the directions say PAST TENSE. *Ran, pitched, jumped,* and *swam* are verbs in the past tense.

When we ask for A PLACE, we mean any sort of place: a country or city (*Spain, Cleveland*) or a room (*bathroom, kitchen*).

An EXCLAMATION or SILLY WORD is any sort of funny sound, gasp, grunt, or outcry, like *Wow!, Ouch!, Whomp!, Ick!,* and *Gadzooks!*

When we ask for specific words, like a NUMBER, a COLOR, an ANIMAL, or a PART OF THE BODY, we mean a word that is one of those things, like *seven, blue, horse,* or *head.*

When we ask for a PLURAL, it means more than one. For example, *cat* pluralized is *cats.*

MAD LIBS® is fun to play with friends, but you can also play it by yourself! To begin with, DO NOT look at the story on the page below. Fill in the blanks on this page with the words called for. Then, using the words you have selected, fill in the blank spaces in the story.

Now you've created your own hilarious MAD LIBS® game!

SENTENCED TO DETENTION PART 1

A PLACE _____

PART OF THE BODY _____

ADJECTIVE _____

NOUN _____

PART OF THE BODY _____

PERSON IN ROOM _____

NOUN _____

PLURAL NOUN _____

ADJECTIVE _____

TYPE OF LIQUID _____

PART OF THE BODY _____

COLOR _____

NOUN _____

TYPE OF FOOD _____

ADJECTIVE _____

NOUN _____

ARTICLE OF CLOTHING _____

NOUN _____

MAD LIBS
SENTENCED TO
DETENTION PART 1

Do you want to end up in detention in (the) _____? Be a
<u>A PLACE</u>

real pain in the _____ by engaging in any of these
<u>PART OF THE BODY</u>

_____ behaviors:
<u>ADJECTIVE</u>

• Hanging a "Kick Me" _____ on the _____
<u>NOUN</u>   <u>PART OF THE BODY</u>

  of _____
  <u>PERSON IN ROOM</u>

• Leaving a sharp _____ on your teacher's chair—*ouch!*
<u>NOUN</u>

• Disrupting classes by loudly slamming _____ into
<u>PLURAL NOUN</u>

  the lockers

• Sneaking a hose into the parking lot and filling the principal's

  _____ car with _____
  <u>ADJECTIVE</u>   <u>TYPE OF LIQUID</u>

• Dyeing your _____ neon _____
<u>PART OF THE BODY</u>   <u>COLOR</u>

• Starting a/an _____ fight in the cafeteria—and lobbing
<u>NOUN</u>

  some creamed _____ at the principal, knocking off his
  <u>TYPE OF FOOD</u>

  _____ hairpiece
  <u>ADJECTIVE</u>

• Jumping up on a/an _____ in the middle of class,
<u>NOUN</u>

  ripping open your button-down _____, and yelling,
  <u>ARTICLE OF CLOTHING</u>

  "I'm _____-man!"
  <u>NOUN</u>

MAD LIBS® is fun to play with friends, but you can also play it by yourself! To begin with, DO NOT look at the story on the page below. Fill in the blanks on this page with the words called for. Then, using the words you have selected, fill in the blank spaces in the story.

Now you've created your own hilarious MAD LIBS® game!

SENTENCED TO DETENTION PART 2

ADJECTIVE _____

NOUN _____

PERSON IN ROOM _____

ANIMAL _____

ADJECTIVE _____

NOUN _____

PLURAL NOUN _____

ADJECTIVE _____

PART OF THE BODY _____

VERB ENDING IN "ING" _____

ADJECTIVE _____

NOUN _____

PLURAL NOUN _____

PART OF THE BODY _____

TYPE OF LIQUID _____

ADJECTIVE _____

MAD LIBS®
SENTENCED TO DETENTION PART 2

Any of these random acts of _____-ness will earn you a one-

<u>ADJECTIVE</u>

way _____ to detention:

<u>NOUN</u>

- Hanging posters with Principal _____'s head on the

  <u>PERSON IN ROOM</u>

  body of a/an _____

  <u>ANIMAL</u>

- Swearing or saying inappropriate things like, "You big _____

  <u>ADJECTIVE</u>

  _____!"

  <u>NOUN</u>

- Spray-painting the desks in the classrooms, the _____ in

  <u>PLURAL NOUN</u>

  the cafeteria, or other _____ school property

  <u>ADJECTIVE</u>

- Coming to class with a tattoo on your _____

  <u>PART OF THE BODY</u>

- Talking or _____ with your cell phone during class

  <u>VERB ENDING IN "ING"</u>

- Flunking a/an _____ test and then forgetting to have

  <u>ADJECTIVE</u>

  your mom or _____ sign it

  <u>NOUN</u>

- Littering the floor with crumpled _____

  <u>PLURAL NOUN</u>

- Dunking a fellow student's _____ in the _____

  <u>PART OF THE BODY</u>   <u>TYPE OF LIQUID</u>

  in the toilet

- Last but not _____, a surefire way to get a detention is

  <u>ADJECTIVE</u>

  to not show up for detention!

MAD LIBS® is fun to play with friends, but you can also play it by yourself! To begin with, DO NOT look at the story on the page below. Fill in the blanks on this page with the words called for. Then, using the words you have selected, fill in the blank spaces in the story.

Now you've created your own hilarious MAD LIBS® game!

MY FIRST DETENTION

PERSON IN ROOM _____

LETTER OF THE ALPHABET _____

NOUN _____

NOUN _____

NUMBER _____

PLURAL NOUN _____

A PLACE _____

ADJECTIVE _____

ADJECTIVE _____

PLURAL NOUN _____

TYPE OF FOOD (PLURAL) _____

ADVERB _____

COLOR _____

VERB _____

NOUN _____

TYPE OF LIQUID _____

CELEBRITY (MALE) _____

VERB _____

MAD LIBS

MY FIRST DETENTION

My name is _____, and today was the worst day of my
PERSON IN ROOM

entire life. Why? I got a detention—my first ever. I don't get

detentions! I'm a straight-_____ student, president
LETTER OF THE ALPHABET

of _____ Council, and the head of the _____
NOUN   **NOUN**

Club. How was I supposed to know that selling friendship bracelets

for $_____ each to raise money for the poor, sick
NUMBER

_____ living in (the) _____ was breaking a
PLURAL NOUN   **A PLACE**

school rule? That's a totally _____ rule! Serving the
ADJECTIVE

detention was not only humiliating—it was downright

_____! I didn't know any of the other _____ in
ADJECTIVE   **PLURAL NOUN**

that room—but one of them smelled like rotten _____.
                                                   TYPE OF FOOD (PLURAL)

_____ gross! And the desk I sat in had some thick,
ADVERB

sticky _____ substance on it that almost made me
            COLOR

_____. Then I got hit with a spit-_____ that was
VERB   **NOUN**

dripping wet with _____. Disgusting! I screamed, and Mr.
                        TYPE OF LIQUID

_____, the detention monitor, gave me a nasty look. I just
CELEBRITY (MALE)

wanted to crawl into a hole and _____ right then and there.
                                             VERB

From ESCAPE FROM DETENTION MAD LIBS® • Copyright © 2013 by Price Stern Sloan,
an imprint of Penguin Group (USA), 345 Hudson Street, New York, New York 10014.

MAD LIBS® is fun to play with friends, but you can also play it by yourself! To begin with, DO NOT look at the story on the page below. Fill in the blanks on this page with the words called for. Then, using the words you have selected, fill in the blank spaces in the story.

Now you've created your own hilarious MAD LIBS® game!

DEEPEST APOLOGIES

LAST NAME _____

ADJECTIVE _____

NOUN _____

A PLACE _____

VERB ENDING IN "ING" _____

COLOR _____

NOUN _____

PART OF THE BODY _____

VERB _____

PART OF THE BODY (PLURAL) _____

SILLY WORD _____

SAME SILLY WORD _____

ADJECTIVE _____

NOUN _____

VERB _____

PLURAL NOUN _____

NOUN _____

ADJECTIVE _____

PERSON IN ROOM (MALE) _____

MAD LIBS

DEEPEST APOLOGIES

Dear Mrs. _____,
      LAST NAME

   I am truly _____ for disrupting yesterday's class on the
                ADJECTIVE

native customs of the _____ tribes of (the) _____.
                           NOUN   A PLACE

It was rude of me to burst out _____ when you
                                  VERB ENDING IN "ING"

explained that the tribal chief wore a/an _____-feathered
                                              COLOR

headpiece in the shape of a winged _____ on his
                                        NOUN

_____. And my decision to _____ in a circle
   PART OF THE BODY   VERB

with my _____ outstretched while chanting
            PART OF THE BODY (PLURAL)

"_____! _____!" was very inappropriate—even
   SILLY WORD   SAME SILLY WORD

though I was only trying to mimic the _____ native dance.
                                          ADJECTIVE

I understand there's a time and place for that kind of _____—
                                                          NOUN

and your class was not it. I know that you _____ very hard
                                               VERB

as a teacher and deserve respect for teaching me and my fellow

_____ every day. I hope you accept my sincere _____
   PLURAL NOUN   NOUN

and believe I will never exercise such _____ judgment again.
                                           ADJECTIVE

Sincerely,

_____
PERSON IN ROOM (MALE)

From ESCAPE FROM DETENTION MAD LIBS® • Copyright © 2013 by Price Stern Sloan,
an imprint of Penguin Group (USA), 345 Hudson Street, New York, New York 10014.

MAD LIBS® is fun to play with friends, but you can also play it by yourself! To begin with, DO NOT look at the story on the page below. Fill in the blanks on this page with the words called for. Then, using the words you have selected, fill in the blank spaces in the story.

Now you've created your own hilarious MAD LIBS® game!

DUNGEON DETENTION

PLURAL NOUN _____

ADJECTIVE _____

NOUN _____

PLURAL NOUN _____

ANIMAL (PLURAL) _____

TYPE OF LIQUID _____

PART OF THE BODY (PLURAL) _____

PERSON IN ROOM (MALE) _____

NOUN _____

PART OF THE BODY _____

PLURAL NOUN _____

NOUN _____

ADJECTIVE _____

ADJECTIVE _____

ADJECTIVE _____

PART OF THE BODY (PLURAL) _____

PART OF THE BODY _____

MAD LIBS®
DUNGEON DETENTION

Did you know that school-age _____ were even given
                                    PLURAL NOUN

detentions back in _____ medieval times? But instead of
                          ADJECTIVE

a classroom, detentions were held in an underground _____.
                                                              NOUN

It was pitch-black because there were no _____ to let in
                                                PLURAL NOUN

sunlight. You could hear sounds of hungry little _____
                                                    ANIMAL (PLURAL)

scurrying in the corners, as well as the *drip-drip-drip* of

_____ from the ceiling. Students were chained by
  TYPE OF LIQUID

their _____ to the walls. Detentions were overseen by
        PART OF THE BODY (PLURAL)

Dark Lord _____. He wore a black _____
            PERSON IN ROOM (MALE)   NOUN

over his face, and had a freakishly scarred _____ and
                                                PART OF THE BODY

warts all over his abnormally large _____. Was the Dark
                                        PLURAL NOUN

_____ a/an _____ freak—or did he just dress
      NOUN   ADJECTIVE

this way to keep students on their best _____ behavior?
                                              ADJECTIVE

Those _____ enough to get stuck in detention with
          ADJECTIVE

the Dark Lord fared well when they remembered these two

important tips: Keep your _____ open and your
                              PART OF THE BODY (PLURAL)

_____ shut!
  PART OF THE BODY

From ESCAPE FROM DETENTION MAD LIBS® • Copyright © 2013 by Price Stern Sloan,
an imprint of Penguin Group (USA), 345 Hudson Street, New York, New York 10014.

MAD LIBS® is fun to play with friends, but you can also play it by yourself! To begin with, DO NOT look at the story on the page below. Fill in the blanks on this page with the words called for. Then, using the words you have selected, fill in the blank spaces in the story.

Now you've created your own hilarious MAD LIBS® game!

DETENTION DIVA

PERSON IN ROOM (FEMALE) _____

ADJECTIVE _____

CELEBRITY (FEMALE) _____

PART OF THE BODY _____

NOUN _____

ADJECTIVE _____

PLURAL NOUN _____

VERB ENDING IN "ING" _____

NOUN _____

PERSON IN ROOM (MALE) _____

VERB _____

ADJECTIVE _____

NOUN _____

PERSON IN ROOM _____

PLURAL NOUN _____

TYPE OF LIQUID _____

PART OF THE BODY _____

ADJECTIVE _____

MAD LIBS®
DETENTION DIVA

My name is _____, and I rule this _____
PERSON IN ROOM (FEMALE)   ADJECTIVE

school as the classy, sassy _____ of detention! I end up here
CELEBRITY (FEMALE)

after school more times than I can count on one _____!
PART OF THE BODY

Usually my crime is forgetting to do my _____ assignments.
NOUN

I mean, who has time? There are only so many hours to do other

_____ things that need to get done, like texting with my
ADJECTIVE

_____ or _____ online or watching my
PLURAL NOUN   VERB ENDING IN "ING"

favorite _____ on television. Luckily, I get a lot done in
NOUN

detention, too. If _____ happens to be there, I can
PERSON IN ROOM (MALE)

sweet-_____ him into doing my homework for me because
VERB

I know he has a/an _____ crush on me. This other
ADJECTIVE

_____ named _____ will sneak out to the
NOUN   PERSON IN ROOM

vending _____ and buy me a can of my favorite
PLURAL NOUN

_____. And sometimes I will make one of the other
TYPE OF LIQUID

kids paint my _____-nails for me—just because I can.
PART OF THE BODY

Now that I think about it, maybe getting stuck in detention isn't such

a/an _____ thing after all!
ADJECTIVE

MAD LIBS® is fun to play with friends, but you can also play it by yourself! To begin with, DO NOT look at the story on the page below. Fill in the blanks on this page with the words called for. Then, using the words you have selected, fill in the blank spaces in the story.

Now you've created your own hilarious MAD LIBS® game!

TEXTING, TEXTING–
THIS IS ONLY A TEXT

PART OF THE BODY _____

VERB ENDING IN "ING" _____

PART OF THE BODY _____

NOUN _____

PLURAL NOUN _____

NOUN _____

VERB ENDING IN "ING" _____

ADJECTIVE _____

NOUN _____

TYPE OF LIQUID _____

PERSON IN ROOM _____

PART OF THE BODY (PLURAL) _____

VERB ENDING IN "ING" _____

ADVERB _____

ARTICLE OF CLOTHING _____

TYPE OF FOOD _____

PERSON IN ROOM _____

PART OF THE BODY _____

MAD LIBS®
TEXTING, TEXTING—
THIS IS ONLY A TEXT

Bored out of your _____ in detention? Well, you
                        PART OF THE BODY

could do some _____ or other homework, but why drain
               VERB ENDING IN "ING"

your _____ when you can use your cell _____
     PART OF THE BODY   NOUN

to catch up with all your best _____ via texting?
                                PLURAL NOUN

JT: 'Sup, my home-_____? I'm _____
                                NOUN   VERB ENDING IN "ING"

in detention right now.

Nick: UR again? What was your _____ crime this time?
                                           ADJECTIVE

JT: I brought a squirt _____ filled with
                                        NOUN

_____ to Miss Marks's class and nailed
TYPE OF LIQUID

_____ right between the _____.
PERSON IN ROOM   PART OF THE BODY (PLURAL)

Nick: LOL! Heck, I'm downright _____ out loud at
                                                VERB ENDING IN "ING"

that one! _____ funny stuff! What do U have up
          ADVERB

your _____ for tomorrow?
     ARTICLE OF CLOTHING

JT: Let's just say it involves a/an _____ launcher
                                            TYPE OF FOOD

and _____'s supersize _____.
    PERSON IN ROOM   PART OF THE BODY

MAD LIBS® is fun to play with friends, but you can also play it by yourself! To begin with, DO NOT look at the story on the page below. Fill in the blanks on this page with the words called for. Then, using the words you have selected, fill in the blank spaces in the story.

Now you've created your own hilarious MAD LIBS® game!

WHO'S WHO IN DETENTION

PLURAL NOUN _____

ADJECTIVE _____

PERSON IN ROOM (MALE) _____

COLOR _____

ARTICLE OF CLOTHING _____

ADJECTIVE _____

PLURAL NOUN _____

PART OF THE BODY (PLURAL) _____

PERSON IN ROOM (FEMALE) _____

PART OF THE BODY _____

PLURAL NOUN _____

ADJECTIVE _____

CELEBRITY (MALE) _____

NOUN _____

ADJECTIVE _____

PART OF THE BODY (PLURAL) _____

MAD LIBS®
WHO'S WHO
IN DETENTION

At my school, the same familiar _____ show up in detention
PLURAL NOUN

so often, it's like they have formed their own _____ exclusive
ADJECTIVE

club. Members include:

- _____: With his long _____ hair and
  PERSON IN ROOM (MALE)   _COLOR_

  his tight-fitting leather _____, this dude is so
  ARTICLE OF CLOTHING

  ruggedly _____ that the female _____ in
  ADJECTIVE   _PLURAL NOUN_

  detention can't take their _____ off him.
  PART OF THE BODY (PLURAL)

- _____: This girl has a really loud _____
  PERSON IN ROOM (FEMALE)   _PART OF THE BODY_

  —and she knows how to use it. If she's not chewing gum and

  blowing _____ in class, she's telling a teacher how
  PLURAL NOUN

  mind-numbingly _____ her class is.
  ADJECTIVE

- _____: Talented at _____-ball but prone to
  CELEBRITY (MALE)   _NOUN_

  getting into trouble, this _____ athlete spends detention
  ADJECTIVE

  flexing and admiring his muscular _____.
  PART OF THE BODY (PLURAL)

MAD LIBS® is fun to play with friends, but you can also play it by yourself! To begin with, DO NOT look at the story on the page below. Fill in the blanks on this page with the words called for. Then, using the words you have selected, fill in the blank spaces in the story.

Now you've created your own hilarious MAD LIBS® game!

PRANKS A LOT

ADJECTIVE _____

ADJECTIVE _____

PLURAL NOUN _____

TYPE OF FOOD _____

ANIMAL _____

VERB ENDING IN "ING" _____

CELEBRITY _____

TYPE OF LIQUID _____

PART OF THE BODY (PLURAL) _____

VERB ENDING IN "ING" _____

ADJECTIVE _____

ADJECTIVE _____

NOUN _____

VERB ENDING IN "ING" _____

COLOR _____

NOUN _____

ADJECTIVE _____

PERSON IN ROOM _____

MAD LIBS®
PRANKS A LOT

Nothing livens up detention quite like pulling a few _____
ADJECTIVE

pranks. Here are some _____ ideas to get your
ADJECTIVE

_____ turning:
PLURAL NOUN

- Order a pepperoni-and-_____ pizza and have it delivered
TYPE OF FOOD

  to detention

- Have your best friend show up dressed in a/an _____
ANIMAL

  costume to perform a/an _____ telegram to your
VERB ENDING IN "ING"

  favorite _____ song
CELEBRITY

- Sneak _____-filled balloons into detention and drop
TYPE OF LIQUID

  them from the windows onto the _____ of
PART OF THE BODY (PLURAL)

  unsuspecting students _____ below
VERB ENDING IN "ING"

- Stage a/an _____ fashion show by cranking some
ADJECTIVE

  _____ tunes on your i-_____ and
ADJECTIVE   NOUN

  _____ down a runway formed from rows of desks
VERB ENDING IN "ING"

- Bring an inflatable _____-headed _____
COLOR   NOUN

  with you, prop it up in the chair next to you, and introduce it as

  your _____ detention buddy, _____
ADJECTIVE   PERSON IN ROOM

From ESCAPE FROM DETENTION MAD LIBS® • Copyright © 2013 by Price Stern Sloan,
an imprint of Penguin Group (USA), 345 Hudson Street, New York, New York 10014.

MAD LIBS® is fun to play with friends, but you can also play it by yourself! To begin with, DO NOT look at the story on the page below. Fill in the blanks on this page with the words called for. Then, using the words you have selected, fill in the blank spaces in the story.

Now you've created your own hilarious MAD LIBS® game!

DETENTION RULES

ADJECTIVE _____

PERSON IN ROOM _____

PLURAL NOUN _____

ADJECTIVE _____

ADJECTIVE _____

ADJECTIVE _____

VERB _____

SAME VERB _____

PART OF THE BODY (PLURAL) _____

A PLACE _____

PART OF THE BODY _____

VERB ENDING IN "ING" _____

VERB ENDING IN "ING" _____

ADJECTIVE _____

NOUN _____

PART OF THE BODY _____

MAD LIBS®
DETENTION RULES

A word of warning to all those who enter the _____
                                                    ADJECTIVE
detention chambers of _____: Abide by the strict
                            PERSON IN ROOM
_____—or suffer the _____ consequences.
PLURAL NOUN   ADJECTIVE

1. Don't be late to detention. Don't be _____ or
                                              ADJECTIVE
   _____, either.
       ADJECTIVE

2. Do not _____ unless spoken to! (Tip: Even if you are
               VERB
   spoken to, it's still best not to _____!)
                                          SAME VERB

3. Keep your _____ to yourself at all times.
                  PART OF THE BODY (PLURAL)

4. If you need to go to the bathroom or to (the) _____,
                                                      A PLACE
   raise your _____ and ask.
                   PART OF THE BODY

5. No eating or drinking! And no _____ or
                                       VERB ENDING IN "ING"
   _____, either.
       VERB ENDING IN "ING"

6. Do not make _____ noises—whether it's with a pencil,
                     ADJECTIVE
   a/an _____, or your _____!
            NOUN   PART OF THE BODY

From ESCAPE FROM DETENTION MAD LIBS® • Copyright © 2013 by Price Stern Sloan,
an imprint of Penguin Group (USA), 345 Hudson Street, New York, New York 10014.

MAD LIBS® is fun to play with friends, but you can also play it by yourself! To begin with, DO NOT look at the story on the page below. Fill in the blanks on this page with the words called for. Then, using the words you have selected, fill in the blank spaces in the story.

Now you've created your own hilarious MAD LIBS® game!

DETENTION SURVIVAL KIT

NOUN _____

PERSON IN ROOM _____

NOUN _____

VERB ENDING IN "ING" _____

NOUN _____

VERB _____

NOUN _____

PART OF THE BODY _____

NOUN _____

PART OF THE BODY _____

VERB _____

ADJECTIVE _____

PERSON IN ROOM _____

PERSON IN ROOM _____

NOUN _____

NOUN _____

NOUN _____

ADJECTIVE _____

MAD☺LIBS®

DETENTION SURVIVAL KIT

My best _____, _____, is a pro at serving detentions
　　　　　　　　NOUN　　　　　　PERSON IN ROOM

and suggests bringing the following items to make it through the hour:

- A/An _____ phone—but don't use it for
　　　　　　NOUN

  _____; instead, use it as a watch, a calculator, or a/
  VERB ENDING IN "ING"

  an _____. And be sure to turn it to "_____"
　　　　NOUN　　　　　　　　　　　　　　　　　　　VERB

  so it doesn't ring.

- An i-_____ to listen to music. Cover up the
　　　　　NOUN

  _____-phones by wearing a hooded _____.
  PART OF THE BODY　　　　　　　　　　　　　　　　　NOUN

- Some tissues, in case you need to blow your _____
　　　　　　　　　　　　　　　　　　　　　　　　PART OF THE BODY

- Blank paper and something to _____ with. Use
　　　　　　　　　　　　　　　　　　VERB

  these _____ items to compose love songs to your
　　　　　ADJECTIVE

  crush, _____, draw a comic strip featuring
　　　　　PERSON IN ROOM

  _____ as the underwear-wearing superhero Captain
  PERSON IN ROOM

  _____-pants, or even do something crazy, like your
　　NOUN

  _____homework
　　NOUN

- A pair of _____-glasses—you might as well look
　　　　　　　　NOUN

  _____ while you're there!
  ADJECTIVE

MAD LIBS® is fun to play with friends, but you can also play it by yourself! To begin with, DO NOT look at the story on the page below. Fill in the blanks on this page with the words called for. Then, using the words you have selected, fill in the blank spaces in the story.

Now you've created your own hilarious MAD LIBS® game!

DETENTION DAYDREAMS

ADVERB _____

PART OF THE BODY _____

ADJECTIVE _____

NOUN _____

ANIMAL _____

NOUN _____

NOUN _____

PLURAL NOUN _____

NOUN _____

TYPE OF FOOD _____

NOUN _____

NOUN _____

A PLACE _____

ADJECTIVE _____

COLOR _____

PLURAL NOUN _____

PART OF THE BODY _____

ARTICLE OF CLOTHING _____

MAD LIBS®
DETENTION DAYDREAMS

Sure, you could do homework in detention, but why ruin a/an

_____ good hour taxing your _____ when
ADVERB   PART OF THE BODY

you could get lost in _____ daydreams like these:
                          ADJECTIVE

- A/An _____ in shining armor gallops up on a/an
          NOUN

  _____, shatters the window with a heavy metal
       ANIMAL

  _____, and rides off with you into the sunset
       NOUN

- A pastry chef named Le _____ wheels in a dessert cart
                                NOUN

  covered with chocolate-covered _____, _____-
                                      PLURAL NOUN   NOUN

  flavored cupcakes, and _____-stuffed pies
                            TYPE OF FOOD

- The President of the United States sends a chauffeur-driven

  _____ to bring you to the White House to advise him on
     NOUN

  how to handle the _____ crisis in (the) _____
                         NOUN   A PLACE

- _____ music fills the classroom, and suddenly you are
     ADJECTIVE

  the star of a music video, flinging around your long mane of

  _____ _____ and shaking your _____
     COLOR   PLURAL NOUN   PART OF THE BODY

  in your leopard-print _____
                           ARTICLE OF CLOTHING

From ESCAPE FROM DETENTION MAD LIBS® • Copyright © 2013 by Price Stern Sloan, an imprint of Penguin Group (USA), 345 Hudson Street, New York, New York 10014.

MAD LIBS® is fun to play with friends, but you can also play it by yourself! To begin with, DO NOT look at the story on the page below. Fill in the blanks on this page with the words called for. Then, using the words you have selected, fill in the blank spaces in the story.

Now you've created your own hilarious MAD LIBS® game!

THE DETENTION SONG

EXCLAMATION _____

SAME EXCLAMATION _____

ADJECTIVE _____

VERB ENDING IN "ING" _____

ADVERB _____

ADJECTIVE _____

NOUN _____

ADJECTIVE _____

PERSON IN ROOM _____

ADJECTIVE _____

ANIMAL _____

NOUN _____

PART OF THE BODY (PLURAL) _____

ADJECTIVE _____

TYPE OF LIQUID _____

VERB ENDING IN "ING" _____

MAD LIBS®
THE DETENTION SONG

_____! _____! I'm once again stuck
<u>EXCLAMATION</u>   <u>SAME EXCLAMATION</u>

In detention—it's due to my own _____ luck!
<u>ADJECTIVE</u>

I'm _____ here 'cuz I was _____ wrong,
<u>VERB ENDING IN "ING"</u>   <u>ADVERB</u>

And I'm singing this _____ detention song!
<u>ADJECTIVE</u>

Woe is me! I'm a/an _____! I'm in some _____ trouble
<u>NOUN</u>   <u>ADJECTIVE</u>

For calling _____ a/an _____ _____
<u>PERSON IN ROOM</u>   <u>ADJECTIVE</u>   <u>ANIMAL</u>

—but it was my double!

Now I'm chained to this _____ when I just want to flee!
<u>NOUN</u>

Woe is me! Woe is me! Woe is me!

I can twiddle my _____—but that's not much fun.
<u>PART OF THE BODY (PLURAL)</u>

How soon until this _____ detention is done?!
<u>ADJECTIVE</u>

Wish I had some flavored _____ to drown all my sorrows—
<u>TYPE OF LIQUID</u>

I hope I won't be _____ in detention tomorrow!
<u>VERB ENDING IN "ING"</u>

MAD LIBS® is fun to play with friends, but you can also play it by yourself! To begin with, DO NOT look at the story on the page below. Fill in the blanks on this page with the words called for. Then, using the words you have selected, fill in the blank spaces in the story.

Now you've created your own hilarious MAD LIBS® game!

DETENTION DUTIES

VERB ENDING IN "ING" _____

VERB _____

ADJECTIVE _____

PLURAL NOUN _____

ADJECTIVE _____

NOUN _____

ADVERB _____

ADJECTIVE _____

PLURAL NOUN _____

TYPE OF LIQUID _____

PLURAL NOUN _____

ADVERB _____

TYPE OF LIQUID _____

CELEBRITY (MALE) _____

PLURAL NOUN _____

ADJECTIVE _____

EXCLAMATION _____

PART OF THE BODY _____

MAD LIBS

DETENTION DUTIES

At our school, detentions don't involve _____
_____ VERB ENDING IN "ING"

in a classroom for an hour. Instead, the principal makes us

_____ around the school. First we head to the cafeteria and
VERB

help the _____ lunch ladies clean up. We have to sweep the
ADJECTIVE

_____ and scrape crusty, _____ tater tots and
PLURAL NOUN   ADJECTIVE

cheesy, _____-topped pizza off the tabletops. It's
NOUN

_____ nasty! Next we go to every _____
ADVERB   ADJECTIVE

classroom and empty the waste-_____. Then we fill buckets
PLURAL NOUN

with _____ and wipe down the chalk-_____
TYPE OF LIQUID   PLURAL NOUN

until they are _____ clean! But the worst job of all is
ADVERB

mopping up the spit, sweat, and _____ in the locker rooms.
TYPE OF LIQUID

If our gym teacher, _____, is there, he makes us go through
CELEBRITY (MALE)

the lockers and remove all the stinky gym _____ and
PLURAL NOUN

_____ underpants crammed in there. _____!
ADJECTIVE   EXCLAMATION

The smell alone makes me sick to my _____!
PART OF THE BODY

MAD LIBS® is fun to play with friends, but you can also play it by yourself! To begin with, DO NOT look at the story on the page below. Fill in the blanks on this page with the words called for. Then, using the words you have selected, fill in the blank spaces in the story.

Now you've created your own hilarious MAD LIBS® game!

NOTICE TO PARENTS

LAST NAME _____

ADJECTIVE _____

PERSON IN ROOM (MALE) _____

PLURAL NOUN _____

CELEBRITY (FEMALE) _____

PART OF THE BODY _____

PLURAL NOUN _____

PART OF THE BODY _____

NOUN _____

VERB _____

PART OF THE BODY _____

ADJECTIVE _____

ADJECTIVE _____

NUMBER _____

A PLACE _____

NOUN _____

VERB _____

PERSON IN ROOM _____

MAD☺LIBS®
NOTICE TO PARENTS

Dear Mr. and Mrs. _____:
LAST NAME

    I am writing to inform you of yet another troubling and

_____ incident involving your son, _____.
ADJECTIVE   PERSON IN ROOM (MALE)

Today he was juggling _____ in the hallway when one
                               PLURAL NOUN

went flying out of his hands and hit the science teacher, Miss

_____, in the _____ and knocked her down a
CELEBRITY (FEMALE)   PART OF THE BODY

flight of _____. She suffered a broken _____
          PLURAL NOUN   PART OF THE BODY

and a bruised _____, and worst of all, she may never
                     NOUN

_____ again! I'm not sure what goes through your son's
VERB

_____ when he decides to pull _____ stunts
PART OF THE BODY   ADJECTIVE

like this. Is everything _____ at home? As a result of his
                         ADJECTIVE

actions, I had to give him another _____ detentions to serve.
                                   NUMBER

The next time, he will be kicked out of (the) _____. I
                                                 A PLACE

would like to schedule a parent-_____ conference with you to
                                    NOUN

discuss our next steps. Please _____ at your earliest convenience.
                                        VERB

    Sincerely,

    Principal _____
                  PERSON IN ROOM

From ESCAPE FROM DETENTION MAD LIBS® • Copyright © 2013 by Price Stern Sloan, an imprint of Penguin Group (USA), 345 Hudson Street, New York, New York 10014.

MAD LIBS® is fun to play with friends, but you can also play it by yourself! To begin with, DO NOT look at the story on the page below. Fill in the blanks on this page with the words called for. Then, using the words you have selected, fill in the blank spaces in the story.

Now you've created your own hilarious MAD LIBS® game!

¡TRAPPED IN DETENTION

PERSON IN ROOM _____

NOUN _____

ADVERB _____

PLURAL NOUN _____

NUMBER _____

TYPE OF FOOD (PLURAL) _____

ADJECTIVE _____

NOUN _____

PLURAL NOUN _____

VERB ENDING IN "ING" _____

PART OF THE BODY (PLURAL) _____

TYPE OF LIQUID _____

PLURAL NOUN _____

PART OF THE BODY _____

ANIMAL (PLURAL) _____

ADJECTIVE _____

CELEBRITY _____

ADJECTIVE _____

MAD LIBS

iTRAPPED IN DETENTION

My BFF, _____, and I host our own web show called
          PERSON IN ROOM

i-_____. It's _____ popular among today's young
      NOUN   ADVERB

_____; in fact, more than _____ people tune in
    PLURAL NOUN   NUMBER

weekly to watch us. Today we are doing our show live from detention.

We have to be careful that Mr. von _____, the detention
                                    TYPE OF FOOD (PLURAL)

monitor, doesn't catch us—or we'll be in very _____ water!
                                                   ADJECTIVE

Luckily he spends most of detention in the _____'s lounge
                                                NOUN

grading _____. We start the web show by doing a little
         PLURAL NOUN

random _____ to loosen up our _____.
        VERB ENDING IN "ING"   PART OF THE BODY (PLURAL)

Then everyone in the room works together with bottles of

_____ and pieces of _____ to make the world's
 TYPE OF LIQUID   PLURAL NOUN

largest spitball—which we promptly hurl at the _____
                                                  PART OF THE BODY

of the kid sleeping at the back of the room. Lastly, we "borrow" the two

albino _____ from the science lab for a/an _____
        ANIMAL (PLURAL)   ADJECTIVE

race—the one named _____ won! Who says detention is a
                      CELEBRITY

bad thing? Frankly, I found it to be pretty darn _____!
                                                    ADJECTIVE

MAD LIBS® is fun to play with friends, but you can also play it by yourself! To begin with, DO NOT look at the story on the page below. Fill in the blanks on this page with the words called for. Then, using the words you have selected, fill in the blank spaces in the story.

Now you've created your own hilarious MAD LIBS® game!

YOUR MOTHER AND I MET IN DETENTION

PLURAL NOUN _____

ADJECTIVE _____

NOUN _____

NOUN _____

PERSON IN ROOM (FEMALE) _____

ADJECTIVE _____

VERB (PAST TENSE) _____

NOUN _____

PART OF THE BODY (PLURAL) _____

NOUN _____

PLURAL NOUN _____

NOUN _____

PART OF THE BODY _____

ADVERB _____

ADJECTIVE _____

ADVERB _____

PERSON IN ROOM (MALE) _____

MAD LIBS
YOUR MOTHER AND I MET IN DETENTION

I was going through some of my parents' old school _____ when
PLURAL NOUN

I came across this _____ letter from my dad proclaiming his
ADJECTIVE

love for my _____—whom he met in detention of all places!
NOUN

To the _____ of my dreams, _____:
NOUN   PERSON IN ROOM (FEMALE)

   My _____ world turned upside down the day you
   ADJECTIVE

_____ in detention with me. I had never seen a
VERB (PAST TENSE)

prettier _____ before. When you sat there with your
NOUN

_____ folded so daintily on the desk, I remember
PART OF THE BODY (PLURAL)

thinking, This is one classy _____. She's not like the other
NOUN

_____! And that's when I knew I had to get your attention.
PLURAL NOUN

Looking back, perhaps folding a paper _____-ball and
NOUN

flicking it at your _____ was not the way to go. Please
PART OF THE BODY

understand I was _____ nervous. I mean, it's not every day
ADVERB

that you meet the person you want to grow _____ with.
ADJECTIVE

   Truly, madly, _____ in love with you,
   ADVERB

_____
PERSON IN ROOM (MALE)

MAD LIBS® is fun to play with friends, but you can also play it by yourself! To begin with, DO NOT look at the story on the page below. Fill in the blanks on this page with the words called for. Then, using the words you have selected, fill in the blank spaces in the story.

Now you've created your own hilarious MAD LIBS® game!

ESCAPE PLAN

PART OF THE BODY _____

NOUN _____

PLURAL NOUN _____

PERSON IN ROOM (MALE) _____

ADJECTIVE _____

PART OF THE BODY (PLURAL) _____

EXCLAMATION _____

NOUN _____

NOUN _____

TYPE OF LIQUID _____

ADJECTIVE _____

ARTICLE OF CLOTHING (PLURAL) _____

NOUN _____

NOUN _____

ADVERB _____

VERB _____

MAD LIBS

ESCAPE PLAN

No one in their right _____ wants to be in detention,
PART OF THE BODY

so you should always have an escape plan in your back _____.
NOUN

Here are step-by-step _____ for one:
PLURAL NOUN

1. Become friends with someone like _____, who
   PERSON IN ROOM (MALE)

   is mechanically _____ and can do anything with his
   ADJECTIVE

   _____.
   PART OF THE BODY (PLURAL)

2. Once detention starts, have someone run into the classroom

   and yell to the teacher, "_____! There's a/an
   EXCLAMATION

   _____ on fire in the boys' locker room!"
   NOUN

3. As soon as the teacher gets there, have your friend activate the

   _____ sprinklers and douse the teacher with
   NOUN

   _____ so she is soaking _____.
   TYPE OF LIQUID   ADJECTIVE

4. Now that the teacher is out of the picture, grab all the

   _____ from the lockers and tie them together
   ARTICLE OF CLOTHING (PLURAL)

   to form a/an _____ ladder.
   NOUN

5. Climb down to the _____ below.
   NOUN

6. You're _____ free! Now _____ for your life!
   ADVERB   VERB

From ESCAPE FROM DETENTION MAD LIBS® • Copyright © 2013 by Price Stern Sloan,
an imprint of Penguin Group (USA), 345 Hudson Street, New York, New York 10014.

MAD LIBS® is fun to play with friends, but you can also play it by yourself! To begin with, DO NOT look at the story on the page below. Fill in the blanks on this page with the words called for. Then, using the words you have selected, fill in the blank spaces in the story.

Now you've created your own hilarious MAD LIBS® game!

EXCUSES FOR WHY YOU MISSED DETENTION

ADJECTIVE _____

NOUN _____

ANIMAL _____

PART OF THE BODY _____

COLOR _____

PART OF THE BODY _____

PLURAL NOUN _____

NUMBER _____

PLURAL NOUN _____

ADJECTIVE _____

CELEBRITY (MALE) _____

NOUN _____

ARTICLE OF CLOTHING _____

NOUN _____

ANIMAL _____

PLURAL NOUN _____

NOUN _____

MAD LIBS
EXCUSES FOR WHY YOU MISSED DETENTION

So many detentions, so little time! Need a/an _____ reason
                                                    ADJECTIVE

that you couldn't show up today? Here are some excuses:

- I had a note from my _____, but my _____ ate it.
                            NOUN   ANIMAL

- I had a sore _____ and _____ bumps
                  PART OF THE BODY   COLOR

  all over my _____ and didn't want the other
                  PART OF THE BODY

  _____ to catch it.
      PLURAL NOUN

- I was on my way when _____ little green _____
                            NUMBER   PLURAL NOUN

  took me back to their spaceship to perform _____
                                                    ADJECTIVE

  experiments on me.

- _____ called and asked if I could be a/an
      CELEBRITY (MALE)

  _____ in his next movie.
        NOUN

- My _____ clashed with the _____ that
        ARTICLE OF CLOTHING   NOUN

  the teacher was wearing.

- A/An _____ escaped from the zoo, and I had to stop it
            ANIMAL

  before it trampled all the _____ in the city.
                                PLURAL NOUN

- I noticed how long the _____ had grown on school
                              NOUN

grounds and decided to mow it.

MAD LIBS® is fun to play with friends, but you can also play it by yourself! To begin with, DO NOT look at the story on the page below. Fill in the blanks on this page with the words called for. Then, using the words you have selected, fill in the blank spaces in the story.

Now you've created your own hilarious MAD LIBS® game!

DETENTION-GETTER
RECORD SETTER

ADJECTIVE _____

NUMBER _____

NOUN _____

PERSON IN ROOM _____

ADJECTIVE _____

PERSON IN ROOM _____

PLURAL NOUN _____

ADJECTIVE _____

PART OF THE BODY (PLURAL) _____

ADJECTIVE _____

PERSON IN ROOM _____

NOUN _____

PERSON IN ROOM _____

NOUN _____

ADJECTIVE _____

NOUN _____

PART OF THE BODY _____

MAD LIBS
DETENTION-GETTER
RECORD SETTER

Nate Nastygram set a/an _____ record this year with
_____ADJECTIVE_____

_____ detentions earned—more than any other
___NUMBER___

_____ in Ridgeway School's history! _____,
___NOUN___   PERSON IN ROOM

a reporter for the school yearbook, talked to him about his

_____ achievement:
___ADJECTIVE___

Reporter: How does it feel to have broken _____'s long-
                                              PERSON IN ROOM

standing record for most _____ earned?
                            PLURAL NOUN

Nate: Well, it feels like a/an _____ weight has been lifted off
                                      ADJECTIVE

my _____ now that I actually did it. I mean, how
   PART OF THE BODY (PLURAL)

awesome and _____ am I?
                ADJECTIVE

Reporter: Yep, you're right up there with _____, who won
                                              PERSON IN ROOM

the most _____-ball games, and _____, who got
            NOUN   PERSON IN ROOM

the highest _____ scores out of the whole class.
               NOUN

Nate: So do I get a/an _____ award for my achievement—
                             ADJECTIVE

a trophy or a medal or a/an _____?
                               NOUN

Reporter: Nope, sorry—just your handsome _____
                                             PART OF THE BODY

pictured in the yearbook.

From ESCAPE FROM DETENTION MAD LIBS® • Copyright © 2013 by Price Stern Sloan,
an imprint of Penguin Group (USA), 345 Hudson Street, New York, New York 10014.

MAD LIBS® is fun to play with friends, but you can also play it by yourself! To begin with, DO NOT look at the story on the page below. Fill in the blanks on this page with the words called for. Then, using the words you have selected, fill in the blank spaces in the story.

Now you've created your own hilarious MAD LIBS® game!

DETENTION MOVIES

PLURAL NOUN _____

ADJECTIVE _____

COLOR _____

PLURAL NOUN _____

PERSON IN ROOM (FEMALE) _____

NOUN _____

NUMBER _____

ADJECTIVE _____

NOUN _____

PERSON IN ROOM _____

PLURAL NOUN _____

ADJECTIVE _____

PERSON IN ROOM _____

VERB _____

NOUN _____

PLURAL NOUN _____

PART OF THE BODY _____

DETENTION MOVIES

Grab a bucket of hot buttered _____ and settle in for
                                    PLURAL NOUN

a viewing of _____ movies about detention.
                  ADJECTIVE

- *Ninjas in Detention*: The _____-clad _____ who
                               COLOR   PLURAL NOUN

  gather in detention every day are really a secret society of ninjas

  who protect the school from trouble. The sweet old principal, Ms.

  _____, is their martial-arts master.
  PERSON IN ROOM (FEMALE)

- *The _____ Club*: _____ kids—including a/an
          NOUN   NUMBER

  _____ athlete, a highly intelligent _____, and
     ADJECTIVE   NOUN

  a troublemaker named _____—gather for a Saturday
                          PERSON IN ROOM

  detention and learn that while they hang out with different types of

  _____, they are actually more _____ than
     PLURAL NOUN   ADJECTIVE

  they thought.

- _____ *Blart: Detention Cop*: This _____
  PERSON IN ROOM   VERB

  -out-loud comedy is about an overweight _____ whose
                                               NOUN

  job is to watch over the rebellious _____ in detention
                                         PLURAL NOUN

  armed only with his wits, a pair of _____-cuffs,
                                         PART OF THE BODY

  and some duct tape.

From ESCAPE FROM DETENTION MAD LIBS® • Copyright © 2013 by Price Stern Sloan,
an imprint of Penguin Group (USA), 345 Hudson Street, New York, New York 10014.